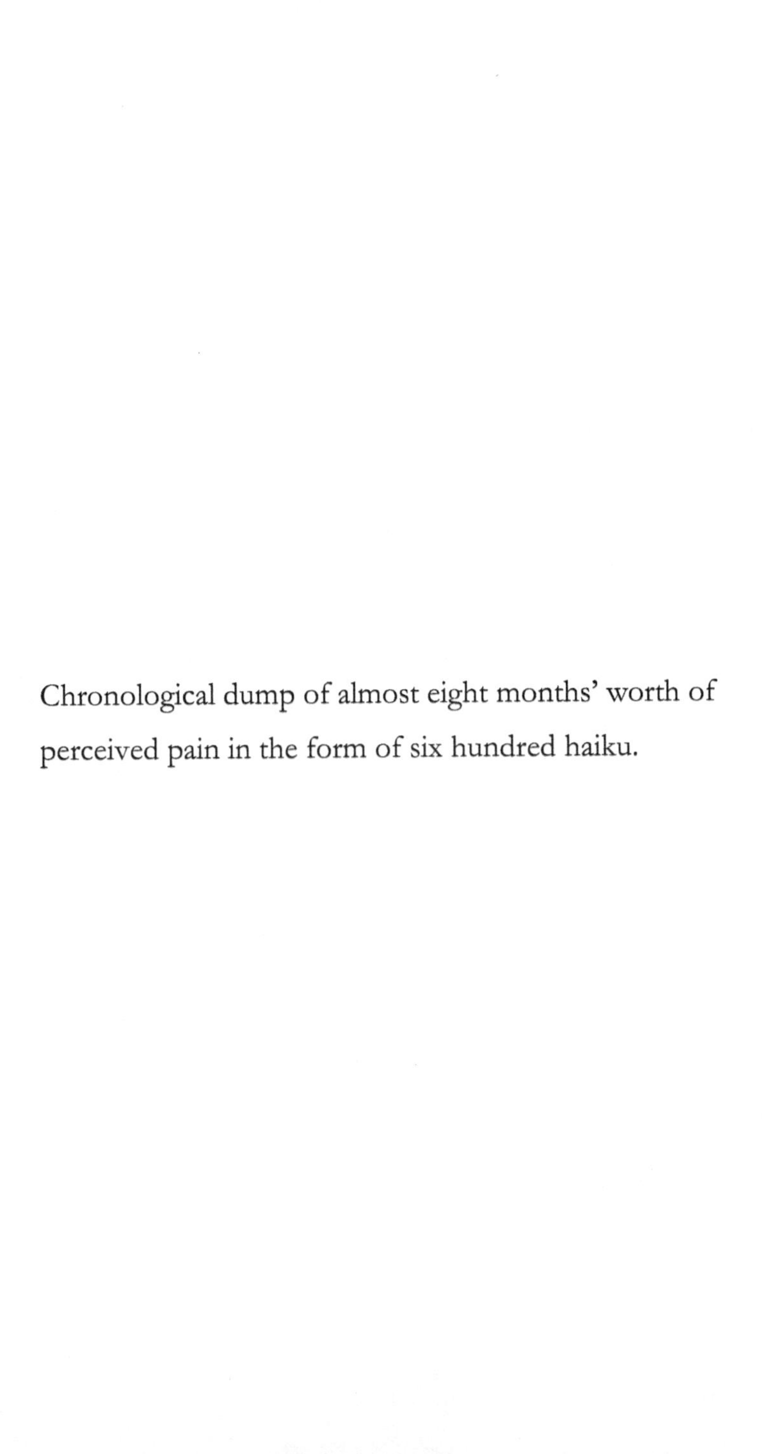

Chronological dump of almost eight months' worth of perceived pain in the form of six hundred haiku.

Thank you endlessly if you existed in my life prior-, during- or post-writing of this; in any capacity – I've learned something from you all.

Apologies if you are upset at me for any of the ensuing words; please find respite in knowing I was pretty angry at myself, too.

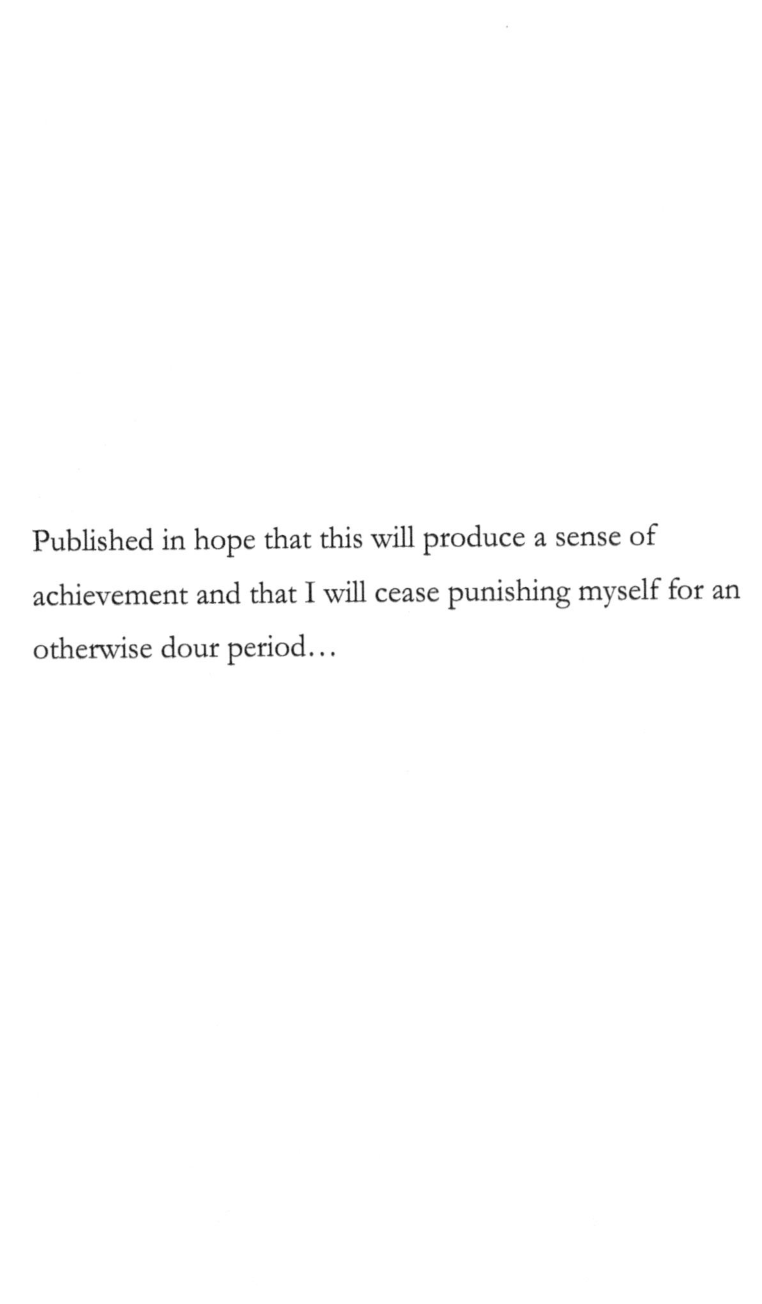

Published in hope that this will produce a sense of achievement and that I will cease punishing myself for an otherwise dour period…

Ruined Your Haiku

17 January 2018 – 01 August 2018

Come and go, like clouds

When will I make it rain down?

When will you leave me?

I cannot contain

How do I stop the spread of

The rot in my brain

These are the hardest

Days that I have ever lived

Hello, Sisyphus

Insecurities;

They will be the death of me

Idly, I watch on.

If all males are me

Listen to me when I say –

Let the females lead

I miss my best friends

I miss when friendship meant most

Now we conceal all

Crying in my room

Ain't bringing you back, I'll cry

On this paper instead

If actions louder

I am quiet as a mouse

I am a coward

Misogynistic

Tv, music, world leaders

We recede decades.

Deep as Atlantis

I tied the rocks to my feet

I will drown right here

How many times can

These feelings be repeated

With true excitement?

Being happy is

Accepting that you cannot

Control other's acts

People always go

But some people never grow

I'm stuck without you

White cars in the street

I see you in all I meet

Missing you = breathing

I haven't cried since

You left me, oh wait, I mean

Not since yesterday.

One-syllable words

(I am multisyllabic)

Are my new best friends

Young gifted and broke –

All the truly talented

Find fortune within

That river of mine

Disembowelled for the white gold

And now we can't swim

- *Amenities lost*

9

I hurt, but I learn

I'm sinking, yet still I rise

I've lost, I'll again.

My mind is bokeh

You are the central subject

Bringing me focus

If I am dirt now

I was rock back then, you ground

Me down; life begins

I have a black dog

She bites those closest to me

I have lost her lead

On her concrete lungs

As this drowsy city sleeps

I found peace, found me.

Listen to the warm

Won't you listen to support?

Please, ignore that voice!

I ruined haiku

Just as white man ruins all

I am so sorry

I love you like I

Am a Montague, and I

Have sealed the same fate

Don't talk, don't feel too

I am so isolated

Classic 'Kiwi' male

Fifty new haiku

Still no closer to my goal:

Getting over you.

This brain is a gift

I just need to convince it

How do I do that?

Simplify my life

One syllable at a time

Rearrange my brain

I, nihilistic

Maybe it's easier to

Cope with pain like this.

Johnny Cash was right

Get a rhythm when you've got those

Awful, wretched blues

I need to defeat

This inward misanthropy

To learn to love me

Family dinner

Silence is on the menu

A dish best served cold

"You change so quickly"

"You think too much, Gabriel"

"…Like walking on glass"

Happiness requires

For some, nothing, for others

The utmost effort

Healing won't occur

If I don't let you go first

I need to want that

You changed my view of

Myself. You showed me true love.

Time to aim inwards.

I cannot control

What means anything to you

What lights your kindling

I could blame you for

Undressing all of my flaws;

I thank you instead.

"You're mean to yourself"

A self-deprecating source

I beat you to it

"I don't know, sometimes

You're your own worst enemy"

Wouldn't you be, too?

Haiku is a form

Of syllabic expression

Seventeen stories

One word to describe

My heart from your fleeting stay —

Rejuvenated.

Self-awareness won't

Scare all those vices away

I must work for it

A cat named Stumpy

He once loved me ceaselessly

I forced my own leave.

Skewed utopia

Rapid gentrification

When will it all end?

When I was with you

I neglected loving me

Now I have no choice

-    *Stuck*

Syncopate my work

I wonder if three lines fit

A lifetime of hurt

Humanity is:

Perpetual mistakes made –

Growth in retrograde

I'm a criminal

Directed towards myself

Most violent of crimes

I did not plan for

Today to hit me like a

Wrecking ball and crane

My views fluctuate

Between deep pessimism

And some manic hope

You were never mine

I just took you out (on loan)

From love's library

Match made by Hades

To expose me to you when

I was not ready

How does everyone

Move on while I remain still

Silently crumbling

I guess this is art

Infinite incarnation

Of my suffering

Tell me, why is it

That when I write of my highs

My lows just seep out?

My engine breaks down

And I find myself stranded

At least once a day

For me it takes more

Than waking with a stranger

To find fulfilment

I am a novice

When it comes to processing

Aftershocks of loss

What's the opposite

Of a Midas touch? Because

I am afflicted

I looked to suffer

So the pain I was feeling

Was validated

Ironic I lost

You through fear of losing you;

I broke my own heart

I sowed a few seeds

Some delicious vegetables

Then never watered.

You were never a

Mirror image of me, why

Did I expect that?

"I hope you're happy –

Everyone knows you deserve"

Everyone but me.

Without bad choices

Well, I wouldn't make any;

I learn so slowly.

Days, months, years soon spent

A Siamese twin named regret

I must amputate

When it rains it pours

When it rains it fucking pours

Where is my jacket?

I am the coxcomb

Destroying all within reach

I seal my own tomb

My art is a crime

Listless criminal offence

Your wall is my heart

Destined to be all

Alone? It's your self esteem

Shouting lies at you

Wiki:how goes from

How to win back your ex, to

How to un-love her.

Everything I write

Is recycled throughout time;

Human suffering.

-     *Plato knew this pain*

I white, white haiku

White people almost spoilt you

I am a white man

Trees are the hair of

Nature's alluring body

Don't touch what's not yours.

I am a list of

Unfinished endeavours. I'm

Only words but ev-

- *Unfinished*

I can't contain me;

My own inhumanity

Trepid to myself

Tim Upperton: Spring

I too ruin everything

Where do we begin?

Dismantle my brain,

Rebuild less self-torturing;

Better engineered.

Some days I am sun;

Some days a shadow in space;

Some days I feel none.

I'm Mariana

The woman or the deepest trench –

Either way asunder.

Can't play and can't sing

Can't draw; no good with my hands.

I guess it's poems.

Your image I peel

Like old gum beneath a seat

It's stuck there. I weep.

People are lonely

In homes, offices galore

Loneliness binds us.

People come and go

They are like the vagrant birds.

I'm one habitat.

I'm fine with regret

It means I tried and failed

Rather that than not

Even if I fail

Always, I'll stay thankful for

Chance *ex nihilo*

Everything ruined

Before I learn anything

I am the white man

I'm in and outside

Imprisoned in my own mind

I swallowed the key

Awful it must be

Somebody had to find them

I wonder who'll me.

The blood in my veins

Each cell of my lost body

Bears only your name

Half a year in what

You said. An entire lifetime

Of my wounds you mend.

You were rainfall to

a drought. You only came when

I was in full flood

I can't wait to feel

Anything other than the

War within my chest

At last, shed this cloak

A weight lifted, I am free

Of possessiveness

Kindness from others

Received makes me feel like the

Pain is all worth it

I've tried tightening

This loose screw inside my brain

Broke the thread instead

I cry the waters

Of a long-lost nation of

Lovers and loners.//

And my tears feed the

Valleys and plains with new life

I seek a true home.//

I seek asylum

But do I really belong

Where is my refuge?//

All internalised

How do I escape a war

Inside my mind?

Pedestals I build

You sit atop my tower;

My crumbling babel

How long until plain

tasks like washing my face don't

Remind me of you?

You are still alive;

You're waves of relentless love;

You're always enough.

Sorrow waits for me

Like a Monday morning on

Sunday afternoon.

Mother sings hymnals;

Birds chirp their melodrama;

My own eulogy.

I love new things wild

I love uncontrollably

I can't control me

Hey man, you don't think

You're worth saving? This poem is

A counteroffer

- *Dear Friend*

Convinced I am wrong

Perhaps my brain ain't so bad

Monochrome living

Poppy lined your arm

A flower planted in skin

As well as my mind

I write a thousand

Lines. A book. To house my words;

Evict you from me.//

When the rent is due

I keep paying up to you;

Landlord of my mind.

Several beds since

Yours. All alone. Since you I

Have not slept well once.

Time is supposed to

Fade your picture hung inside

My shipwrecked houseboat

I'm that submarine

Kitschy parts tossed to create

A sane semblance

Life is: falling for

The girl of your dreams who then

Turns around and leaves.

Remember when you

Said we felt like soulmates, well,

Isn't love just great?

You're never going

To wear me across your chest

Again, are you, Hon?

Inescapable.

You are inescapable.

I'm blind in a maze.

Let me watch you rub

That cream on your face. Let me

Wrap you in my legs.

How? How is it done?

How do you stay happy there?

Or anywhere else?

Somewhere someone is

Moving on. Somewhere else is

A lover struggling

"I'd rather be low

Than lowered into the ground"

I'm not so sure now.

You showed me beauty

In mist rolling over hills;

Grey caressing green.

I want to capture

The moon. To magnify in

Awe. The moon and you.

Sick to my stomach

Whenever I think of you —

With grief, not disgust.

In an age of lust

Am I the erroneous

For wanting to love?

Alone in my own

Head. I don't like this part of

Town. Please pick me up.

I want to be more

Than a blink of your ice eyes;

Decision's not mine.

Is it loneliness

Causing small acts of kindness

To make hearts quiver?

I had an affair

Cheated on you with the worst

Of my ugly brain

Even when I'm high

I'm low. And even when you're

There, you'll soon be gone.

There are no sunsets

In black and white. Only clouds.

Welcome to my eyes.

Time is infinite

In that those months spent as one

Will cost a lifetime.

Sometimes I'm crazy;

Desperation drove me to

Losing all I knew.

Breaker bay washes

Over me. Your waves never

Cease. You're relentless.

Antidepression

Is a fucking myth, I think.

I can't change a thing.

Letting go of me

Was facing up and saying

I was not your want.

-      *Or need.*

If these are fragments

Of my memoirs, I hope they

Never reach your eyes

-    *When taking your own life seems more than just an option.*

Self-dependency

Seems a green mile's walk away

Death or peace found first?

My friends summited

Everest. I'm drowning in

Mariana's trench.

Nature: my cure-all.

From heartache to loneliness

Birds and trees relieve.

I'm afraid drugs will

Blunt the best of me. Is this

Overreacting?

You don't have to be

Stone. You are warmer than that.

Please let me see it.

Let me be the first

Thing you forget. While you will

Occupy me 'til death.

You embraced me

And my worries melted away

You are her mother.

Awkward. Fumbling with

My tongue and sentence structure.

Self-conscious at best.

This world is too cruel

For someone so sensitive

That a look can kill.

Is life more than just

Shaping and reshaping of

Ephemeral dust?

You are the sum of

All the best and worst traits of

Everyone you've met.

Plane crashed with no land

In sight. Never learned to swim

Either. Feeling doomed.

Connection requited?

Or was it only hormones

And love's psychosis?

Forget about me

Faster than a midwinter

Sunset. Lost in dark.

I would hang my head

If I had the guts. Instead

I hang it in life.

Cheese fell off the board

I never had any cheese

Lost my crackers too.

How else do I stop

These thoughts from occurring than

By ending my life?

I just don't know if

I am capable living

Another fucking day.

Do you ever want

To open your car door on

A highway and fall?

Wishing for a crash

A tragedy to make my

Dire mind up for me.

I want to jump but

For the rope to break. Is this

Me dreaming for help?

It does not matter

What she wants. All that matters

Is that it's not me.

If life is a box

Of chocolates, then I'm a

Vegan. They've all milk.

Unsurmountable

The pain associated with you,

Me, and your leaving.

Is there a feeling

More cumbersome than that of

Unrequited love?

Is this hole somewhere

I can climb out of if I

Have built my home here?

Your vessel still moored

In my harbour. Stripped of goods.
59

I can't lift anchor.//

Reason exported.

I've tried to make you set sail.

Pleas gone unanswered.

Girl, I never knew

You could save me and leave me

In coincidence.

Obsession's iron chains

Are never crafted in pairs.

My brain's gift to wrists.

If self-sabotage

Was a sport, I'd stand atop

Mount Olympus.

How you just appeared

And hurled me to novel heights

Now that's love to me.

I love you enough

To hope you never in life

Have to feel like this.

All the heat my love

Emitted, couldn't thaw a

Correct decision.

To a depressive

Camus' question is all that

Occupies the mind.

You are magnetic

My mind is laced with lead. It

Gravitates to you.

If you are jealous

You are not ready to love

'til you love yourself.

The wolf runs down the

Deer almost every damned time.

I long to be prey.

Ever since a teen

Only future I have seen –

Death by my own means.

I'm singing along

To the tune of your ghost gone

Forever haunting.

Things that mean the world

To you, won't ever mean that

Much to someone else.

Blizzards in your eyes

You freeze my mind every time

The pairs of ours meet.

Own worst enemy

Making you go was in line

With kamikaze.

How weak am I that

Losing you could be all it

Takes to ruin me?

Me and you might be

Open flames to gasoline

I guess we will see.

And you present me

To the world as a memoir

Of what you don't need

Everything I thought

About our relationship

Was probably wrong

Tonsil tennis 'tween

Newlymets. To bridge the rift

Your departure left.

You are an idol

Your words are swords through my heart

And I stand unarmed.

Such a voracious

Appetite for the skin stretched

Over your new bones

You could be my nurse

As I lie in A & E

My recovery.

You set fire within

But you extinguish yourself

And I'm left blackened

Ash is most fertile

New life will triumph darkness

From your death I rise

Put them in a book

Send it to all of my friends

See how I suffer

I thought you were great

We just let each other down

A looped self-portrait.

I have a sweet tooth

For your amphetamine touch

You boil blue my blood.

Imagination.

Images of you swirling;

Now all I possess.

Tonsil tennis will

Not clear the mess in my head;

It's fun nonetheless.

Sometimes you can love

With a looming expiry

You love nonetheless.

My heart, exhausted

And shattered. Yet still it wants

Nothing but to love.

And I'm frustrated

Because I still have stories

I had hoped to write.

How do we know if

Our hearts have lost sensation

Mental burns patients

'Losing you is like

Cutting my fingers off' – I

Have lost all feeling.

-   *Turnover*

Our 'shared peace halts time

In a catatonic trance'.

I believe your heart.

-   *Stubborn light*

I loved as if you

Were the last person on earth –

There's another way?

First moments in bed

Let's ravel our limbs as one

A human pretzel

Why do I do this?

Canonise all who show me

Any decency

Does anybody

Else ever hurt us? Or do

We do it ourselves?

Illusory: I

When amiability sparks

Infatuation

Illusory: I

Infatuation rapid

Almost every time

A cruel lesson to

Run back to pain right after

Pain has consumed us

I should not write you

Further into my heart than

You already are.

And still nothing moves

Me quite like your pale face, or

These days – the ghost of.

Was it you or the

SSRIs? Perhaps you

Are one and the same.

Why do I wrestle

Every single day with this

Existential angst?

You control the earth

Like an insecure lover.

Manipulative.

I can't wait to love

Myself crazy. Like I love

Everybody else.

If only it was

As easy as increasing

Our serotonin

Sometimes I need you

Sometimes I need to love you

I always want both

Sometimes I want you

Sometimes I want to love you

I always want both

Mental health is no

Excuse for treating someone

With lesser respect

-   *Yours or theirs*

I can't push aside

A tooth to let another

Grow. It just won't move.

If I were a plant:

Cross melon with broccoli;

I'm melancholy.

Pray to God or the

Universe. But you are your

Only solution.

How can I expect

To breathe freely when there is

Still a gaping hole.

I don't think a girl

will make me feel a king

Walking down streets again.

Hand in hand was like

Holding the Amazon's trees

And tasting their breath.

We are all nothing

To someone. I hope they are

Not your everything.

These syllables swirl

But there's nothing I can say

You haven't yet heard.

Each morning my mum

Left a note. Each morning I

Died before I rose.

We started in a

Straight line and ended up in

Separate ways: K

\-   *Like the first letter of your name.*

Rescue me. I want

You to. Even though I know

It's all up to me.

I can barely kill

An ant. While other hands crush

Civilisations.

People can die and

Their heart keeps beating. While yours

peters to an end.

Tonight I have died

One hundred times inside. I'm

As good as stale bread.

I am Saturn on

The walls of your mansion home

I devoured us both.

-     *Goya*

If I could paint my

Mind's state, it would be graphic:

A train wreck in wake.

Selfish syllables

I write of this pain as if

No one has seen worse.

Dear reader, I hope

You can take something from my

Self-indulgent words.

I write pain because

It was all I had wired my

Brain to know to feel.

The culmination

of millions of years of life

You're a survivor.

Your whole lineage

Passed on to you life; survived.

You're a miracle.

Your eyes and pursed smile

Carry so much past baggage

Let me shoulder some.

Your flaws are canyons

In a vast landscape. I laud

Your topography.

You are a band-aid

Can I keep you on even

After my wound heals?

I am another

Crooning citalopram kid

These words are my mic.

- Dangers

Why, when I close my

Eyes, do I crave concrete from

Thirty stories high?

My brother, made most

Of a shit hand of cards, he

Has a boxer's heart.

This one, my sister,

Whose passion and loss of words

Give mine their purpose.

Final sibling, mad.

I only wish one day to

Halve your resilience.

You are atoms of

Dinosaurs and diamonds and

Stardust and mountains.

My mind's atmosphere

This anthropogenic gas

Pollutes my vista.

I talk and write of

My feelings every day. I

Am no less a man.

If being a 'man' is

Violence and self-neglect

I would rather not.

Your heart was foreign

I never translated your

New language of love.

If I never love

You illusory, perhaps

It's me maturing.

We can't find escape

In a person and expect

It to be sustained.

-    *Falsity*

Stop global warming

Stop pretending to love me

Stop global war, please.

-    *From the earth to us*

Her eyes like raindrops

Each glint from an ocean of

Deeper emotion

Her jet blue eyes were

Like SSRIs to the

Tides of my tired mind

Brief snippets of my

Syllabic misery and

Sometimes frantic joy.

Days like this make me

Realise all that I've missed

Was less than I have.

-    *A good day*

I've learned more in your

Absence than I ever would

Have in your presence.

Each time we touched there

Were big-bangs. You created

Galaxies in me.

Six years is a long

Time to learn that you don't love

Someone as you thought.

When the one person

You look forward to seeing does

Not want to see you

- *Sheepish*

Anxiety is

A trebuchet flinging thoughts

Over the ramparts.

You, my gardener

Resigned and left as the weeds

Choked the rest of me.

Riverside markets,

Green lakes and black beaches; the

Waters of our love.

I kept burying

Myself. You got tired always

Unearthing me, dead.

How can someone else

Cruelly mean more to us than

Our own golden lives?

There are two humans

Those inherently selfish

And those who give all.

I've roamed these dark streets

For a decade, as if they

Will give me reason

Everything I see

Seems a surreality

Through my clouded lens

If I walk down all

The darkest streets, perhaps they

Will enlighten me

I can't feel God in

Anything. I can't even

Feel my feelings.

People care. Why do

I keep convincing myself

That nobody does?

Love is another

Medicine to which you will

Become resistant.

Remember please not

My imperfect persuasions

But my love beyond.

Why does nobody

Else think these suburban homes

Are ridiculous?

- *Minimalise*

You gave me Modest

Mouse, Milo, and increased my

Mental awareness.//

Awareness better

Phrased: mental fragility.

Either way, increased.

- *Thanks, I guess.*

Why does excitement

From attraction veil any

Rhyme or good reason?

I will make the same

Promises already made

And not before kept.

You were my first love

And very nearly you were

My last ever love.

Don't leave me alone

With my thoughts and me. I can't

Survive my own mind.

How do I change my

Routine from being solely

Self-deprecation?//

These are the worst of

Wasted days, living in my

Waste of a good brain.

'Kill yourself' is not

The solution. Then again,

Who am I to judge?

Found a girl, lost self.

Lost girl, forced to find myself.

Found new girl, who knows.

You're struggling to live

In this world of busyness

'Just try harder'. Ugh.

I ask you to do

Things daily. I don't enjoy

My own company.

    -    *Why would you?*

I walk past hundreds

Of mansions each nightmarish

Day. These are not dreams.

Why is your car so

Angry? Matter of fact, why

Are you so angry?

    -    *Fuel*

"You change so quickly

It is like stepping through glass"

It is all broken.

I still write of her

More than all else. Until that

Changes, I'm not well.

We're soulmates, you think?!

New love is illusory.

You snapped out of it.

Who broke you, yourself?

Did you love unrelenting

Before knowing how?

A storm can open

Gates, while all around is left

Destroyed in its wake.

Beauty can end up

Hideous if you let it.

Don't give it the chance.

Said she wanted to

Be there as a friend, then we

Never spoke again.

For whom do I write

If I think of you always

With nothing to say

My infernal love

Yours a lot more tepid –

Trepid opposites

I've cried but I won't

Die here. I won't die here. I

Won't. Might cry. Won't die.

Everything you said

To me was ephemeral

It felt eternal.

Your caramel skin

Tempting me in grey cotton

How could I resist?

Pain, a currency.

I would trade yours away for

My love. A fair deal.

I locked your car door

Then yanked the wheel off that bridge

You're sinking with me.

What would you do if

I died? Would you even bat

A precious eyelid?

I want to visit

Places where a Topo map

Is our sole comfort.

Knowing you need to

Get out of bed but being

Your own mind's captive.

\-   *Manifested*

Your skin is its own

Poem, sung to me by a

Chorus of seraphs.

Points of difference

Make people more attractive;

The unexpected.

Your skin seized my eyes

From your décolletage to

Your innermost thighs.

Love, idiotic;

It lacks any scent of sense;

Joyous pointlessness.

When you shared, you shared.

All shades of you, like stained glass;

Your colours were vast.

Do you neglect tasks

Until they overwhelm you?

Then we are the same.

Your anxieties –

Statues – do they make of you

When pleading movement?

I was one-five years

Acting edgy, who knows why;

Now two-three, still edge

-       *Why?*

I remember now

That I have lost my living

My dreamscape returns.

You were the sweetest

But your actions screamed perceived

Antonyms of you.

Your skin a roadmap

My fingers tourists. I wish

To see every street.

Beach-based piggybacks;

Rainy private lounge concerts;

Your love is all shapes.

You're the air in my

Fucking lungs. I just wish you

Could breathe for me too.

Acacia Brinley –

She grew up; married, a kid.

What have I done since?

Remember that night:

"I think I'm in love with you"

I guess you thought wrong.

When you said I was

One of your favourites. I

Felt valued, for once.

My brain is mashed peas:

Green, but mostly a gross mess

No one wants to eat.

Sometimes I sit on

Skype, waiting for you to call

Like we would each night.

-     *Once-upon-a-time*

Why do I only know

How to love like a flame and

A dust cloud of flour?

Attraction is you

Looking good trying on my

Old grandpa trousers.

You were a first draft

I wrote, was pleased with, and then

Never touched again.

Can you ghost ride life?

Or does it only work with

Cars? I can't function.

Never thought I would

Still be writing the same wars;

Syllabic cycles.

-    *Four months on*

I tend not to club

I have a sharp wit meaning

I'd likely get clubbed

If the sun is a

Blood orange or ruby red

How do I peel it?

I am my own Sphinx

Except instead of my nose

My whole head fell off.

How is it six months

Of your love can hold more weight

Than six years of hers?

To people I hurt:

I was only neglecting

My own pain. Sorry.

-       *A regretful bully*

I never followed

Your mum on Instagram, I

Knew this would soon end.

Repetitions of

Everything we felt, until

Sparks aren't imagined.

-    *Finding someone else*

I will suffocate

Everybody that I love

Until there are none.

This may burn faster

Than the setting solstice sun

In late afternoon

Without a rope from

Which to hang, I look instead

To these pills in hand.

I'm fine. My writing

Is one big caricature

(I'm dying please help)

-        *I'm fine.*

Nails through my temples

The entire day except when

I briefly see you.

My cat loved me more

Than I have been loved before

I left him with her.

When a bullet through

Your head would be the sweetest

Fucking pain relief

- *Delirious*

Sometimes you can't choose

Who you fall in love with or

When your heart freezes.

My sisters are now

Climbing the steepest steps, while

I can't find my socks.

-    *Parenthood*

There is no treasure

In this shipwreck. There is no

Thing worth your effort.

You wanted someone

You thought I was. When I changed

You fell out of love.

-     *Revealed*

Nobody cares for

Me the way I care about

Them. It's common sense.

Light for once, for what

Seems like the first time in months.

A blood moon eclipse.

If I were a dog

Julien Baker – Go Home

Would play in my head.

-    *You told me of a game you play when you'd see dogs and imagine what
music played in their heads. I guess humans have their own anthems too.*

This medication

Messing with my dreams, making

Odd ordinary.

Rigor mortis of

My entire fucking brain

What have I become?

Still wear your jacket

As if it's nothing to me

And still I wear you.

I have to force my

Brain to stop writing sad lines

When I want to sleep

Most people move on

They don't wear others around

Their neck like love's slaves.

Sometimes making one

Happy is not enough to

Make one want to stay.

Life without you will

Never be as vibrant as

It was when with you.

How will I escape –

Without dying – this mess I

Have made for myself?

If I die from this

Know that you are the strongest

Person I have met.

I think of you as

A brilliant, somewhat manic,

Unpolished genius.

Quarantine my brain

From those it wants to infect

I host this virus.

How high is enough?

Will I regret my choice as

Soon as I step out?

If you look for a

Reason, after long enough,

They will choose to leave.

-     Stop the deprecation

I thought I had grown

But I am now more fragile than

I have ever been.

-     Growing pains

If home is where the

Heart breaks then my home is in

Every bed I've stayed.

-    *HFN*

I just want to be

Able to rest my head when

It hits the pillow

A margarine house

Will not survive the summer

It will melt with heat

-    *Foundations*

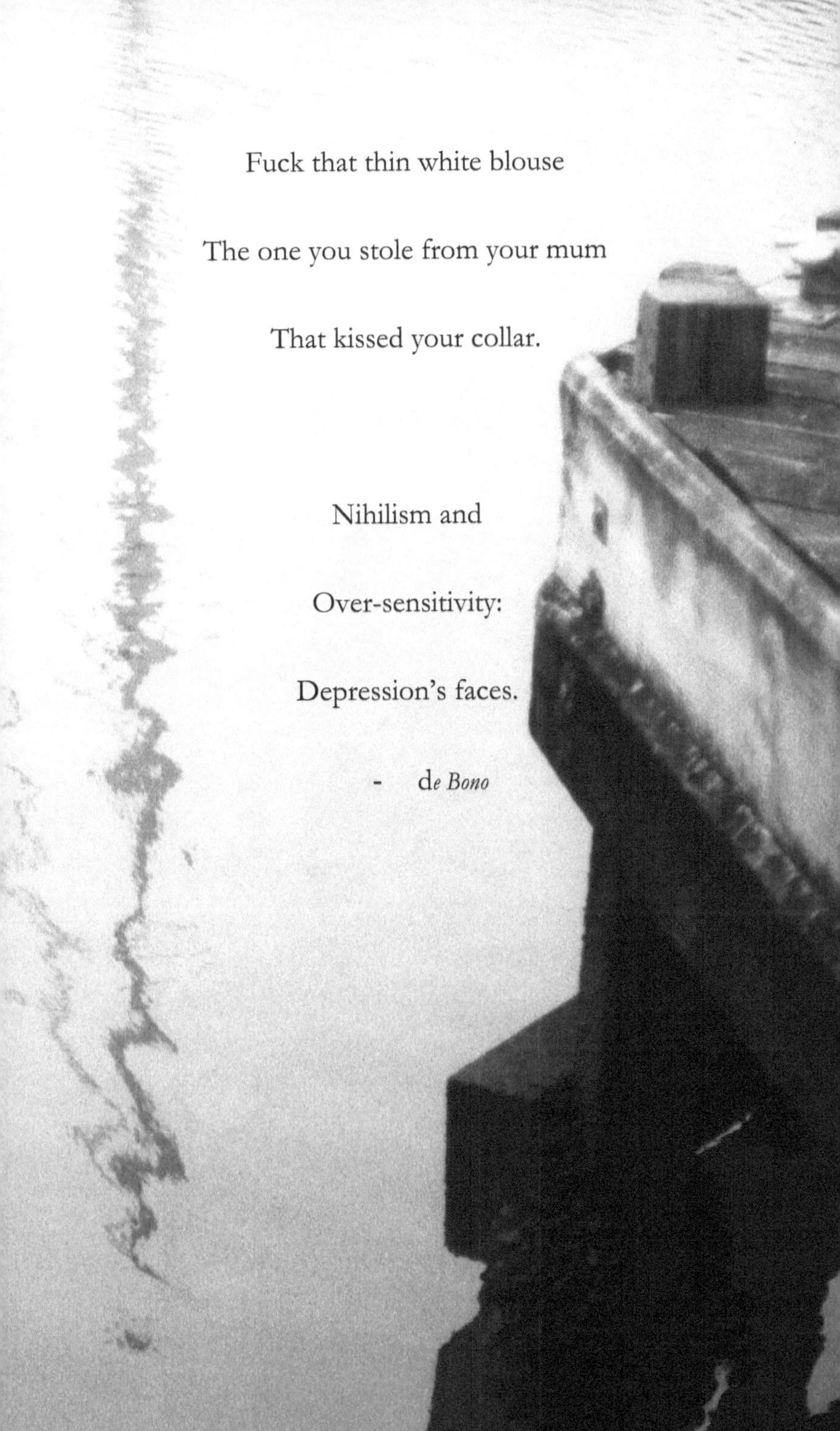

Fuck that thin white blouse

The one you stole from your mum

That kissed your collar.

Nihilism and

Over-sensitivity:

Depression's faces.

-    de Bono

Do you think of me?

Ha ha ha, hilarious.

I don't cross your mind.

If Instagram was

A measure of wellbeing, my

Empty feed tells all.

Lately the daydreams

Have been a stake puncturing

Straight through my sternum.

Are you ever so

Bored that taking your own life

Seems more rewarding?

"I've come to see that

I now care as a friend would"

Never spoke again.

As a kid I would

'Ask too many questions' so

Now I am silent.

To save this, I would

Have given everything. You

Did not do the same.

My tactic seems to be

Make you fall for me and then

Find it out from there.

- *Naively inconsiderate | Narcissistic.*

It's not honest to

Convince you to want me when

I don't want myself.

A relationship

Should be between two adults

Not one and a kid.

-    *Emotional immaturity*

The end. It's like the

Beginning, just without the

Hope and happiness.

I am monoxide.

Watch you inhale my highs, then

Watch me dim your eyes.

"I'm not looking for

A boyfriend right now" – she was,

It just wasn't me.

-    *Some people know what's good for them | admirable*

Sometimes a routine;

A circadian rhythm;

Remedies the brain.

Beagle puppy eyes;

Freckles scattered like fall leaves;

Nature in your face.

You don't need to know

What's wrong with me unless you

Care genuinely.

My brain unsteady

Flicking like film slides between

Potential futures

You're an oasis

In my desertified brain;

Life through arid soils.

Another day gone

Waiting to be wanted by

Those looking elsewhere.

In a matter of

Days watch me go from your all

To anonymous

Am I more than my

Sexual actions or do

They define all I'm?

Latency between

Mistakes and learning seems as

Permanent as death

I dream of making

Ardent love to you but I

Was only some fun.

It's great going from

Top of your list to one of

Many left unread.

-   Letters

Girl, you may just have

Convinced me killing myself

Is not the answer.

-    *Learning from others*

My mind; Huguenot

My actions; French Catholics

Bartholomew's day.

Four failures later

I think it's finally time

To cut my cursed hair.

I am an Arctic

Ice sheet. I am melting and

You just can't change that.

The breath in my lungs

Wished to first pass through your own

Hands, I'll have to change.

You can give me love

Without falling in love with

My frayed sutures.

-    Friends

And my body is

Two-day old socks that no one

Wants to touch again.

Tasting you just made

The fantasies in my head

All the more frequent.

You are unique in

That I just can't predict where

Conversation goes.

My body is a

Used condom. You no longer

Have any use for.

-	*Discarded*

There's more war than sane

In my brain. More hate than peace

For the skin I'm in.

You wanted who you

Thought I was. Now you don't want

Anything of me.

If you make me feel

Untouchable then how bad

Could we really be?

-    *You & I*

In cliff-lines that stretch

Beyond horizons; footprints

Swallowed by oceans.//

Where I found your love

During a peculiar time

Regifted me life.

If I cut my hair

Will I forget you ever

Ran your hands through it?

-    *Cut*

I can't help but think

My naivety leaves me

Prone to succubi

Most men are pigs, but

Succubi are genderless

Men too are abused.

I will massage you

Until you ache no more, so

You might sleep better.

Stalagmites of ice

Climbing in front of my eyes

Then melting away.

\-   *When dreams transition to nightmares*

I want either to

Be alone or with you. There's

No good in between.

Pirouettes in sand

By silver sea. Did I kill

Us or only me?

- *Rushed*

Spent the year in a

Room the size of a cell and

A mind just as cruel.

- *Trapped*

I survived nightmares

For a month of bliss with you

Now what do I do?

- *Dosage*

I will never be

Enough. I want you, I don't

Care if it's not love.

Am I any good

To the universe like this?

Five new moons, still shit.

I'm not your lover.

Just another pushover

You had your way with.

Life is a series

Of questions we've pondered but

We leave unexplored.

Life is a game show

Or a carnival stall game

There are no winners.

Life is an exam

And I'm failing quite badly;

It's harder than maths.

Placing cocoa in

Warm rice milk. Like watching days

Without you dissolve.

I'm a masochist

Searching for hurt, preventing

Love from requiting.

Am I a victim?

Or am I an incubus?

Or can I be both?

Love is Bermuda

Triangles. You find it once

Then you go missing.

Your affection was

Phenological in that

It changed with the wind.

Death wrestles with sleep

Both untoward in coaxing

Me into their grasps.

I pray in my life,

Or posthumously, someone

Finds my words soothing.

Life is finding a

Moonlit girl who beams then just

Changes phase and wanes.

Thousand foot broken

Home. Welcome to the great New

Zealand dream, folks.

More garage spaces

Than content humans. Hello,

Bourgeois New Zealand.

Metal detector

Of yours beeped. Unveil me; just

A rusted tin can.

How do I love my

Maniacal mind when all

I love leaves me blind?

I brushed my teeth too

Hard and my gums bled. I did

That to you as well.

I would change schedule

For you. You wouldn't move a

Muscle in return.

-        *Differing values*

From all the pain I

Was feeling; perhaps you were

Just a distraction.

It's nice to know that

I can't count on you even

Though I wish I could.

\- *When you think you need someone is right when you need to learn to deal with things on your own.*

You're telling me it's

Not romance when I look in

Your eyes and combust?

I can't tell if you're

Afraid of intimacy

Or afraid of me.

Your moments recalled

In pale monochrome. Where has

All the colour gone?

-     *Feelings fade, memories stay.*

Gypsy tapestries

Remind me how colourful

Time with you can be.

-     *Your mind is a mandala I could never draw*

Spent a year eating

Soup. I guess you really are

What you fucking eat.

This kid in a film

Asked: 'you fundamentally

ill?' Maybe I am.

- *Manchester by the Sea*

Sex lost its meaning

When I lost my love and it

All became too much.

- *Now I try to fuck my way to love*

I will not blame you

I will try not to blame me

Sometimes love just goes.

I'm the first scene in

The Secret Life of Walter

Mitty, on repeat.

She smiles when I call

Her the sweetest thing ever;

My niece, not lover.

I'm letting go of

A friendship that never gave

Me what I needed.

-   *A difficult decision*

Expectations are

The rope that loops into a

Noose by my own hands.

Sport is good as a

Remedy where alcohol

Probably won't work.

\- *Exercise*

Nobody will be

Everything I want them to

Why can't I see that?

\- *Grow up.*

Every mall entered;

Instead of consumer's dreams

Brings sober disdain

'There is no-one new

Around you.' Like clean rivers

And our native birds

- *Tinder the environmentalist*

If a man ever

Made you feel finite, then he

Is just not worth it.

- *Myself included.*

Bread and hummus, Kai

Iwi pumice, we made a

Month somehow endless.

- *Gone*

I have enough friends

That don't mean anything to

Me. I want meaning.

- *Deeper friends*

Sometimes I think I

Am more woman than man. I

Am gentle gentile.

- *Kiwi Blokes R Not Us*

She loves me; she loves

Me not. She loves me not. She

Loves me not. She loved.

-      *Petals*

If night is a cave

Anxiety must be a

Grizzly bear in wait.

Tarried memories;

A brain full of tar today,

Tomorrow the same.

-      *What changes?*

A green mantis can

Look like a leaf so why can't

I just be happy?

- *Is it really that elusive?*

I didn't love you

Just loved moments that we shared

And what we would do.

- *Love confused.*

Be who you want, babe,

Don't let anyone who calls

You babe make you change.

- *Relationships don't always encourage growth.*

Thirty forth in my

List of friends I have messaged;

First in my wishes.

They will never find

As much meaning in things that

Are dearest to you.

-   *Differences.*

Your ambivalent

Moon pulls my tides more strongly

Than noticed at first.

I pontificate

Projecting my own self-hate

Onto our love's grave

-    *I am no better but I should know better.*

You are a fig tree

Feeding your inhabitants

With plenteous fruit

-    *Foundation of the forest*

I don't need you in

My life, but that doesn't mean

That I don't want you.

-    *I am my own sun*

I am what's left of

A cult of sensual beings:

Tragic romantics.

I am the pizza

Man. The one waving his sign

That nobody reads.

- *Intersection*

My friends saw me when

My heart was aflame. Now they

See me extinguished.

- *At least you don't see me like this.*

I am romantic

I gave away everything

For one bus ticket

    -   *First poem about you//progress stinted*

I'm a harbinger

You're a flood in my future

I won't prepare for.

    -   *Knowing and doing nothing.*

Like lava in a

Crater lake swallowing soil

You make my blood boil

    -   *Intellectual lust*

I would bend over

Backwards if it meant that I

Got to see your face

-     *Won't you reciprocate?*

I wonder if it

Is possible to fall in

Love for just a night

Sadness, anger, guilt

Atop derelict buildings

Local music scene

-     *Artist run spaces*

Mouths full of our doubts

Arms carry each other's dreams

Our hearts shout and scream.

- *First meeting*

My heart is breaking

In airplanes and airports I

Find myself again

- *Familiar*

Teeth meeting fingers

Like two sides of a zipper

Blissful, I kiss her

- *Lips*

Why do we as men

Expect women to follow?

We can't make them come.

Short and sharp kisses

Feel like multiple stab wounds

I am your victim

- *Love's violence*

'I don't want this to

Ever end.' Five seconds on

And your alarm rings.

- *When life gets in the way of love.*

I will never be

Silenced by courtesy, no,

I will speak freely.

-    *Honesty*

My heart is a globe

And it writes of your beauty

Wherever you go.

-    *Gabriel on Lacroix*

There aren't plenty of

Fish left in the sea for me;

White society.

I loved everyone

That I fucked. And that started

When you fucked me up.

When will I learn to

Be a man? When will I learn

To repress feelings?

- *I'm doing it wrong*

I love you, like I

Wish I didn't, but like I

Knew I always would.

- *Pathetic/prophetic*

You romanticise

My fear of oceans; drowning

Me in affection.

It's just repeated

Feelings, man. Do we ever

Tire from feeling them?

You skin on my skin

Warms my days like Napier's

North-westerly wind.

I love with every

One of my DNA strands

With you it's the same//

    -    *The way I love*

I love like seraphs

Greeting Jesus to heaven

With you it's the same//

    -    *The way I love (ii)*

I love as science

Or religion, either way

I love you the same.//

    -    *The way I love (iii)*

"I want to play with

Your hair forever but my

Arm gets really sore"

-    *Francesca*

I hold you close as

My compass but I will still

Probably get lost.

-    *Shaky needle.*

It's a blue Monday

But it's Tuesday, or Thursday

I've lost track again.

I am full of it;

If 'it' is lovely poems

For lovely women.

My atrium is

Currently flooded with light

That is your doing

Let me reach inside

Of your body, like a clown

Into his black hat

\-   *Rainbow sheets*

Money is nothing

To me, in comparison

Love is everything.

Am I wrong? Or just

Wrong for you? Are we in love?

Or is this just new?

-   *Questioning*

You are a ladder

I built you up so, vine-like,

I could cling to you.

Love at first sight? Nah.

But I believe in falling

In love at first night.

You are everything

I could have been if not for

Who I came to be.

- *Drawn to me.*

You don't care about

Me, you just like that I care

So much about you.

- *Pine*

I eat crusts to save

You the good bread. That's all you

Need to know of me.

Your touch is the string

In Eros' bow and love

Unto me you fling.

Rod McKuen, Tourettes,

And Tim Upperton. All are

Poets as well males.

-     *We aren't all (always) pigs.*

And maybe this is

A strain of sick; medicine

Will never quite fix.

-      *Cure me*

How much will I let

You get away with as my

Heart slowly decays

-      *Sometimes love is too patient.*

Your escapades from

Which you escape justice leave

Me crying in sheets.

-      *Am I justified or just insecure?*

I can't offer you

Money for your attention

So am I worth it?

Nothing is right and

Nothing is wrong. Just please don't

Murder anyone.

I crave a stake through

My heart like a vampire

Longing for a cure.

   -   *Seemingly eternal*

I brought a pheasant

To a falconry meet, yeah —

It's been a rough week.

To you I was just

Elevator music while

You were my penthouse.

-     *Suite.*

You have done nothing;

Nothing wrong, but nothing right,

As sorrow takes flight.

-     *Don't blame yourself.*

I feel everything

And nothing all at the same

And it's exhausting.

- *Thin skin.*

Six months, half a world

Sometimes love is too patient

Waiting for a girl

- *She's not coming back.*

My heart is breaking

These days with the changing of

The weakest of winds.

- *Over again.*

You love me a lot

I believe it, but in love

With me, you are not.

- *Difference*

If love's influence

Is addictive, then I am

A problem thinker.

- *Triggers*

Under a maroon

Moon in torpid countryside;

Reacquaint ourselves.

- *Distance*

Your friends must think I'm

An absolute fool to be

Writing you poems.

I have not launched one

Thousands ships for you, does that

Make me wise or fool?

-    *Ask Faustus*

I have never been

As infatuated as

At your fingertips.

-    *A shame I wasn't ready*

Who ever did know

I could fervently love you

And still you would go.

-      *'Love ain't fair'*

White sheets got too hot

When laced with sorrow's thick fleece

So you chose to leave.

-      *In search of New Manchester*

Fumbling through this life

About as effectively

As a deaf-blind bat.

-      *Sensory ineptitude*

You loved me like a

Plaster loves a wound before

You tore yourself off.

There are others that

Will love you like a morning

Dew clings to petals.

- *Don't settle.*

Is a poem still

honest if it lends itself

To melodrama?

- *Am I?*

Lily pad heartbreak:

I jump from heart to new heart;

A frog that can't swim.

- *Dysmorphia*

I am worth more than

You ever perceived. Why did

You not value me?

- *Insecurity — yours or mine?*

Thought I was at my

Worst. Turns out I was only

At the precipice.

- *Wheels*

Is a lie still a

Lie if you are trying to

Protect somebody?

-     *Grey*

Don't let me pull you

Down to the nadir of my

Relentless despair.

I admire your clout -

To put yourself first while I

Peppered you with doubt.

How will I shake it;

This sardonic existence

As heavy as sin.

- *Encumbered*

Let go of what you

Can't control if you struggle

To live with yourself.

- *Empty your hands*

One searing fear is

That I will be survived by

Nobody at all.

- *Epitaph*

I don't want to die

It would not solve anything

But I want to try.

Tried grinding but my

Trucks got stuck and I ended

Up flat on my face.

-    *Bailed*

I learned love from you

When our peace held time in a

Catatonic trance.

-    *Your words, your company.*

It is only me

Because no one else is there

For you this second.

-    *I'm not special.*

It's almost time in

Our narrative, where you fly

While I crawl behind.

-    *Metamorphosis.*

Depression is not

Competition; I once was

A participant.

-    *Social media bloodstains*

You shouldn't worry

For deciding to leave this.

For us it is best.

Unbleached paper for

Unbleached skin. Your forgiveness –

Where do I begin?

-    *Generational wrongs*

Eat my nightmares with

Self-same arms. Vomit my dreams,

Escape this self-harm.

-    *Self care*

Half a year, despair

Snapped by realisation;

Lucky to be here.

-       *thanks.*

If hurt is heartfelt

Can art be artificial

If my art is hurt?

-       *Ponder | Sonder*

From ataraxy

I acted with laxity

It's reckless from me.

Thought I knew better

But this time I refuse an

Inward vendetta.

-    *Pain or change, at least I have an option.*

Pain or change, I am

One lucky boy, you see, I

Have the choice between.

-    *Others aren't so lucky.*

Life ain't weightlifting;

The heavier the better

Does not ring true here.

Eight months of nothing –

Always been a slow learner;

Time to do something.

-       *A clock won't tick again without fixing what's wrong.*

The moon was bleeding

So we kissed ferociously

Searching for meaning

-       *Lunar lessons*

Billie Eilish is

My Billy Idol she is

A giver of gifts.

The damage of words

Often irreparable

Even innocent

- *Unnoticed*

I have been selfless

I have been a narcissist

I am still learning

- *I'm sorry.*

Square actions and round

Emotions. Depression and

Obsession take hold.

Retrograde living

Burning before building and

Lust before loving.

-    *We can't blame the planets.*

We all self-destruct

You don't have to be manic

To damage yourself

A toll bridge from yours

To my heart, I made you pay

You knew from the start.

-    *Much too wise for my trials*

Your crisp skin glistens;

At Eden's fruit they gawk, though

Never were you theirs.

-      *You are your own*

Treading water for

Eight months of the year. Time to

Force myself to swim.

Frantic flights, quick nights.

Virgin sex, coconut cream.

In the wake of dreams.

Marine Reserve

Imprisoned within

My room and my mind, alas,

Key is in my hand.

Your pain is valid

Just please, I beg, try not to

Indulge like I did.

- *There are other options.*

A toast for all the

Women who gave up on me;

Your worth fathomless.

- *Tough love works, eventually.*

You spent a year in

The Ivy League. I'm more proud

Of you than of me.

My phosphenes provide

Sophrosyne, now I must

Source them within me.

-      *Open eyes*

Some New Zealanders

Still do not want refugees;

Selfish sovereignty.

-    *Xeno*

'She said fuck me like

You love me.' Instead I fell

Accidentally.

-    *Cake*

I wish that I could

Liken the white atop waves

Never relenting.

-    *Soon.*

NPW – the next one's yours.